COPYRIGHT 2021 NAUTICAL FISHER COLORING

ALL RIGHTS RESERVED. NO PART OF THIS BOOK MAY BE REPRODUCED IN ANY FORM BY ANY ELECTRONIC OR MECHANICAL MEANS INCLUDING PHOTOCOPYING, RECORDING, OR INFORMATION STORAGE AND RETRIEVAL WITHOUT PERMISSION IN WRITING FROM THE AUTHOR.

TEST YOUR COLORING MEDIUM IN THE BOXES

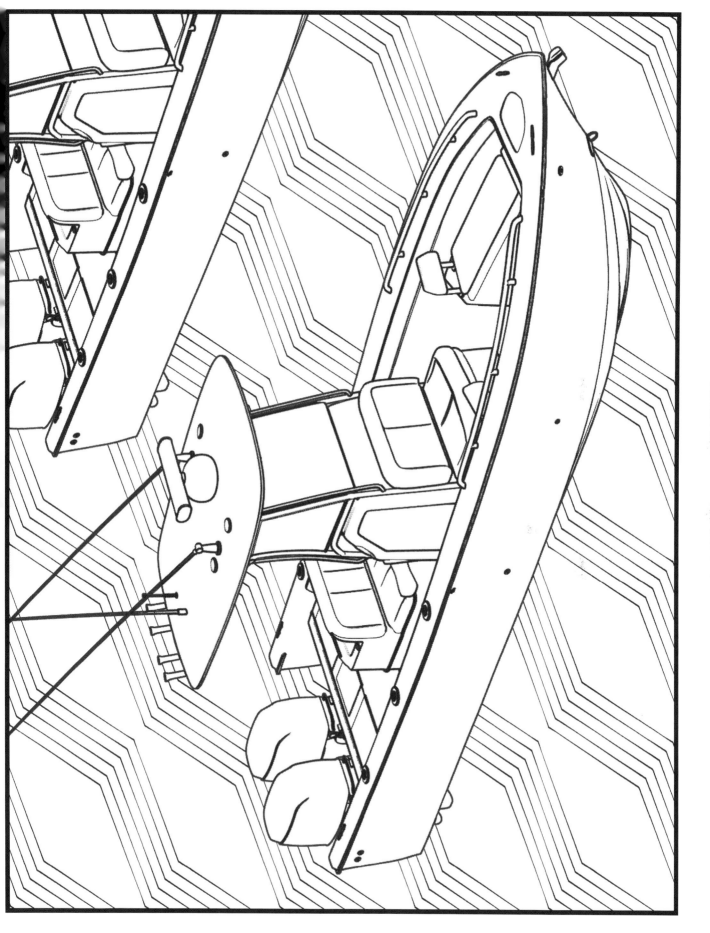

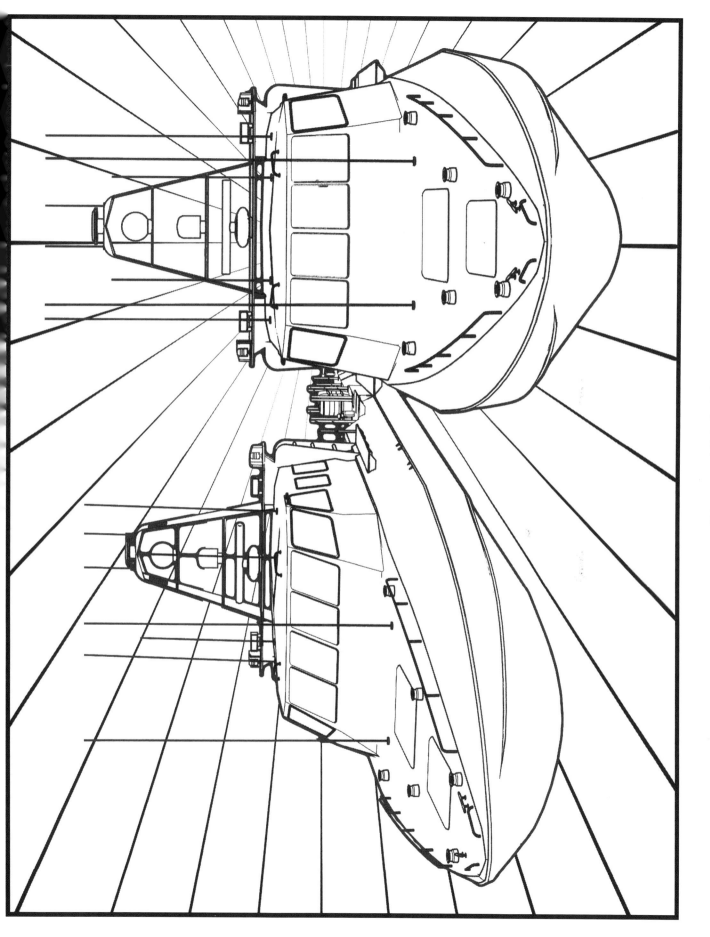

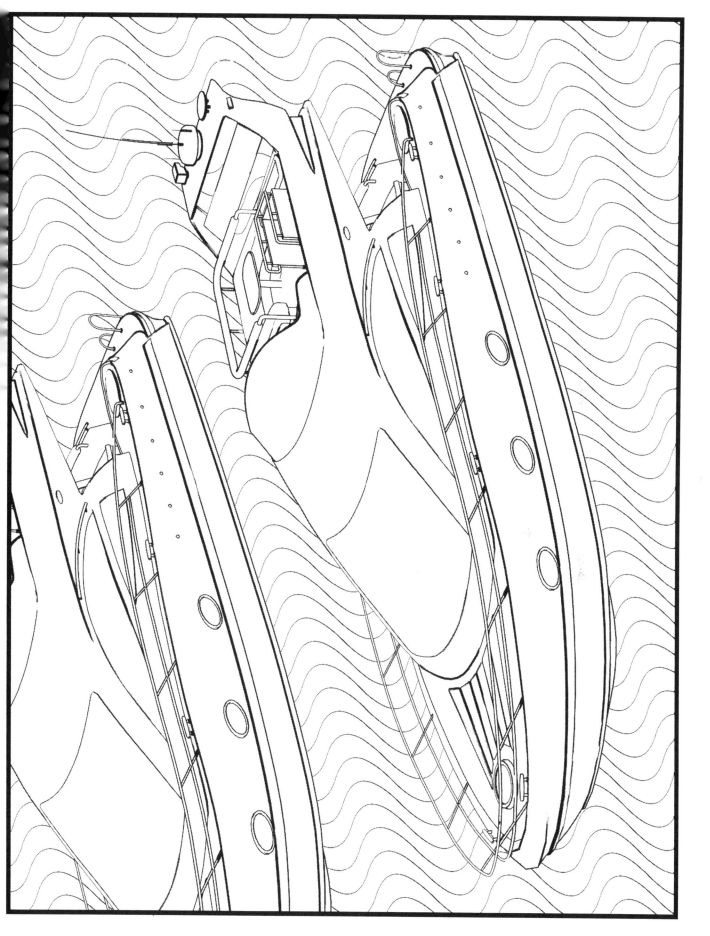

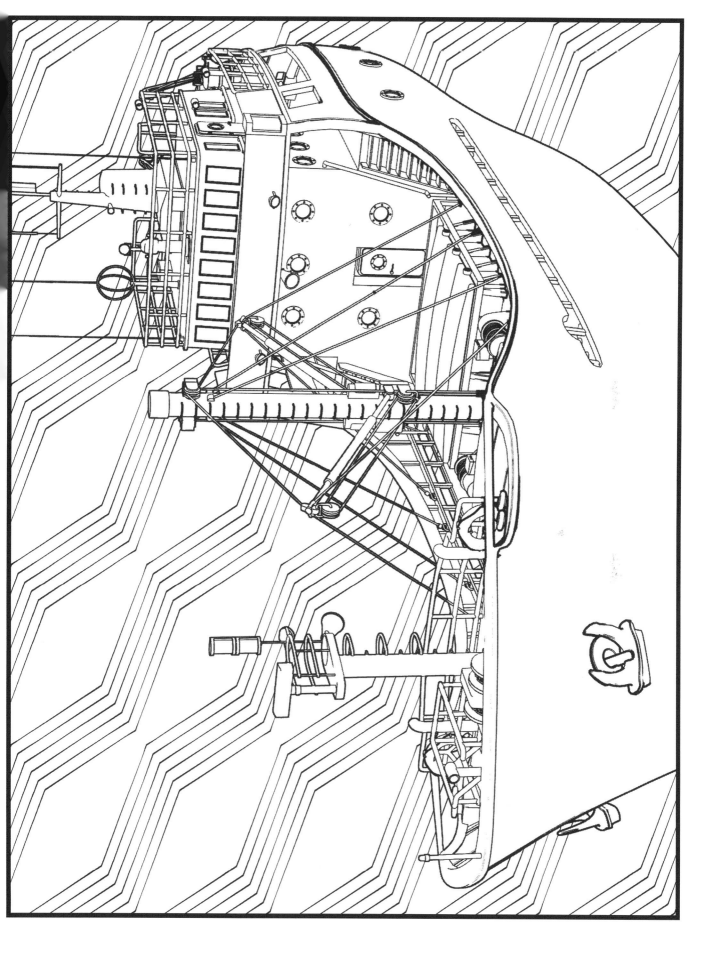

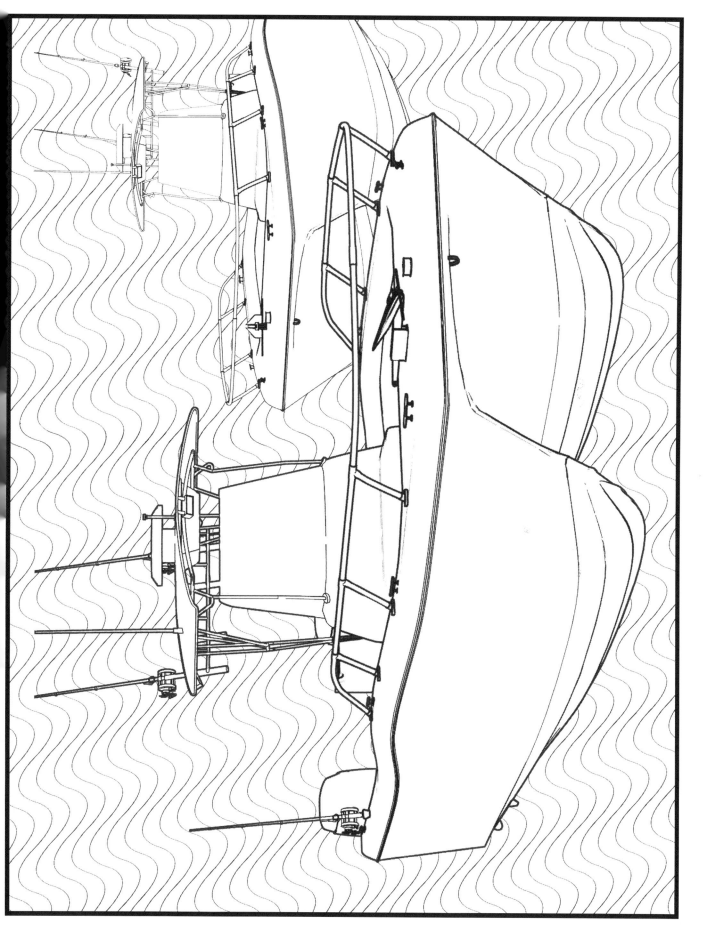

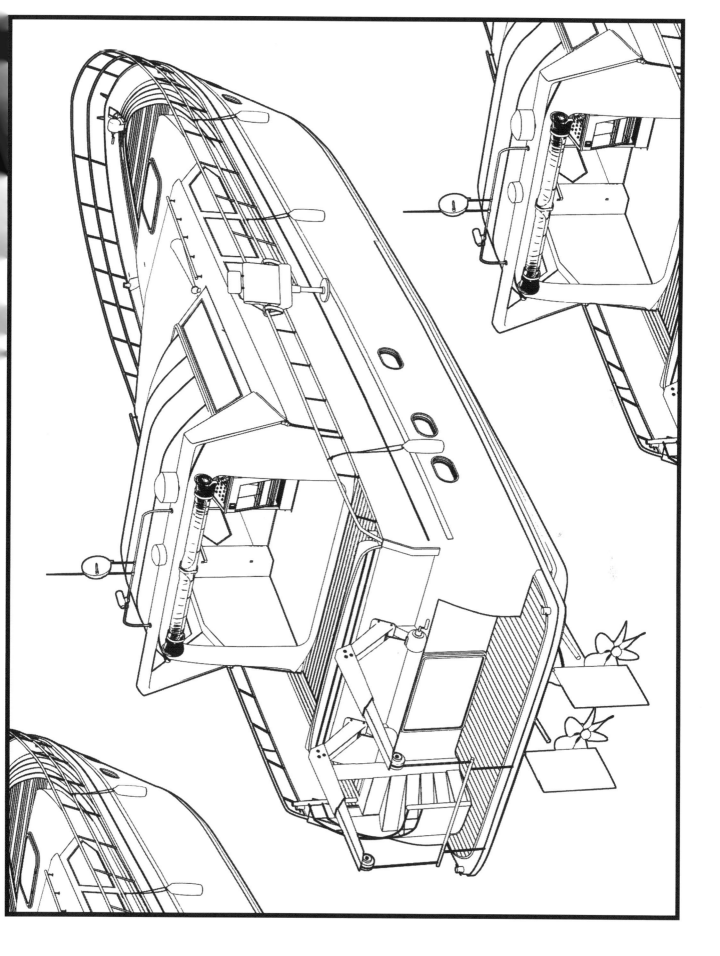

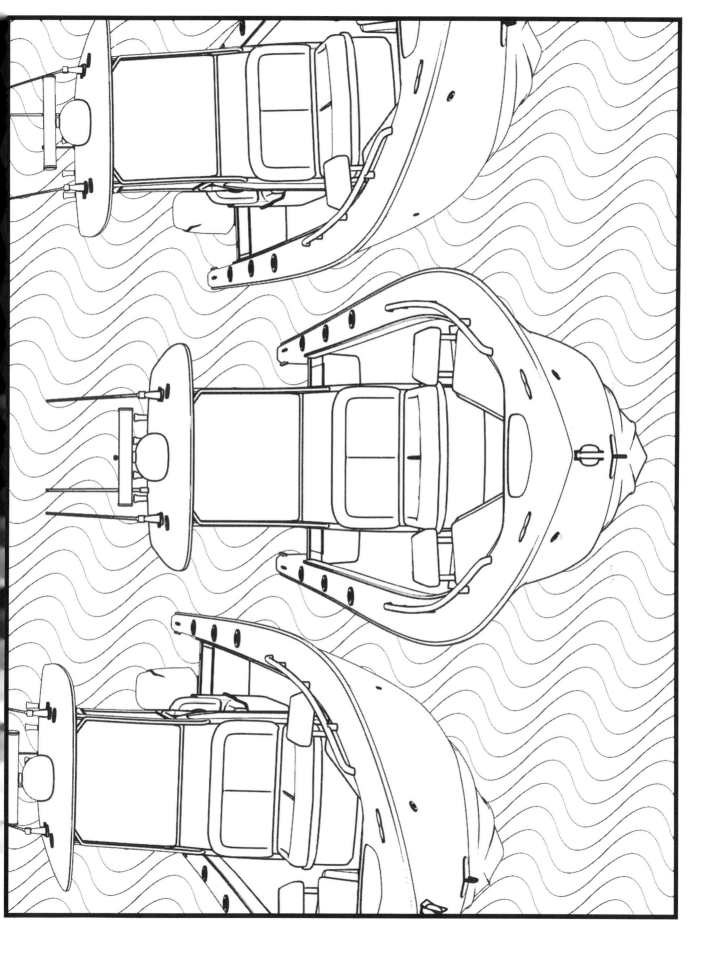

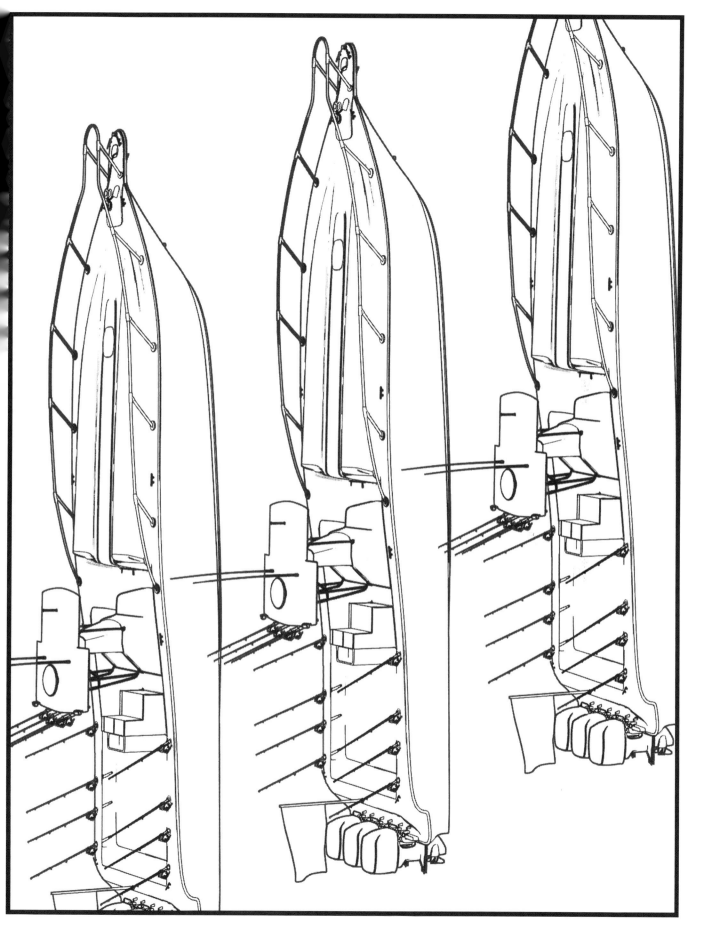

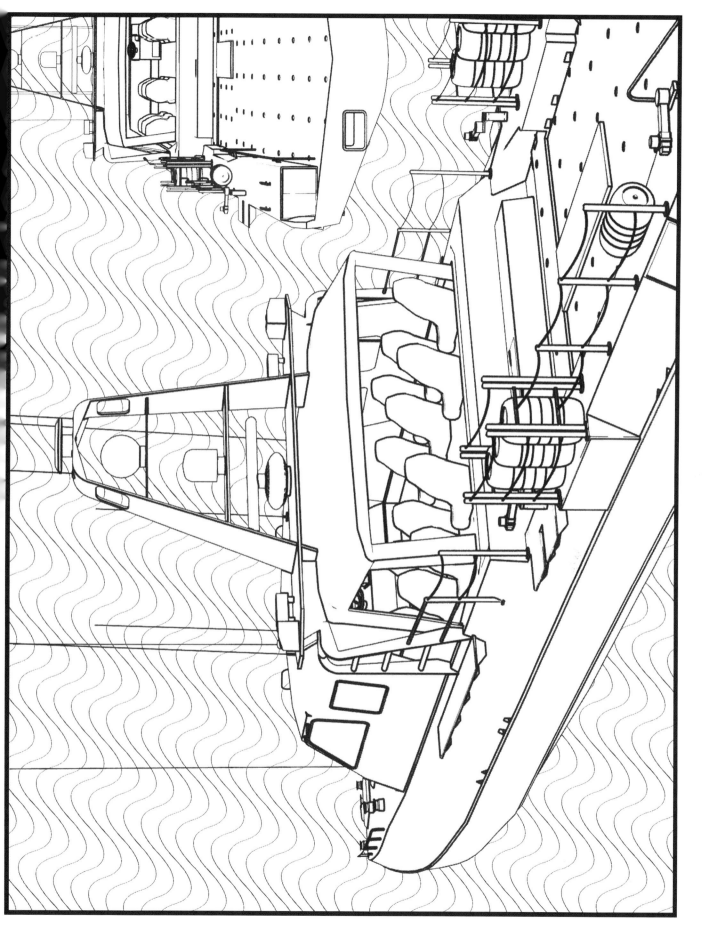

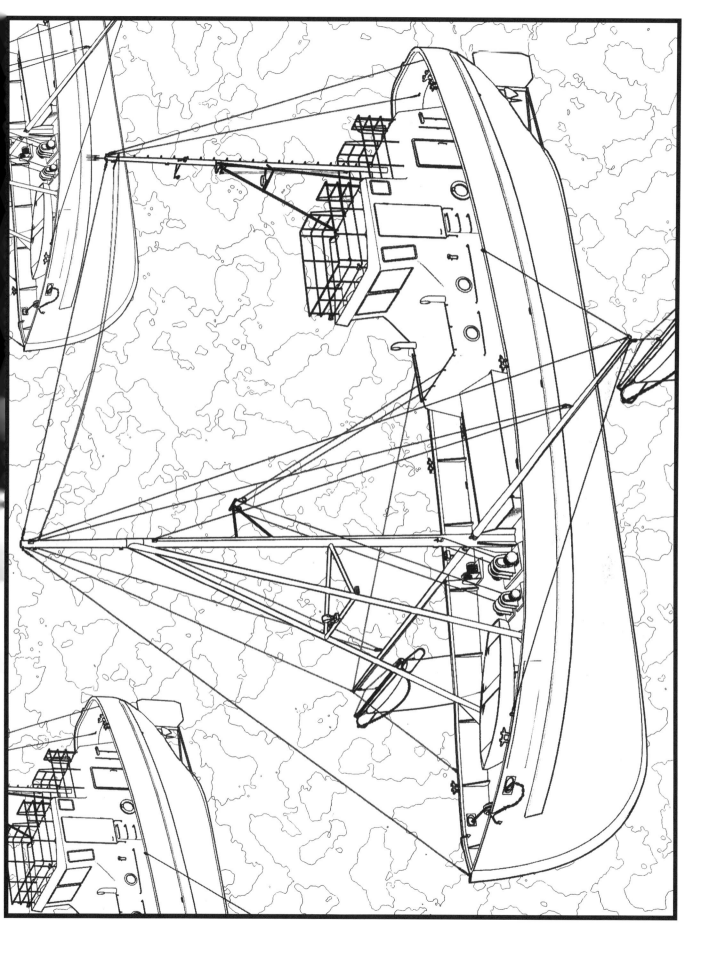

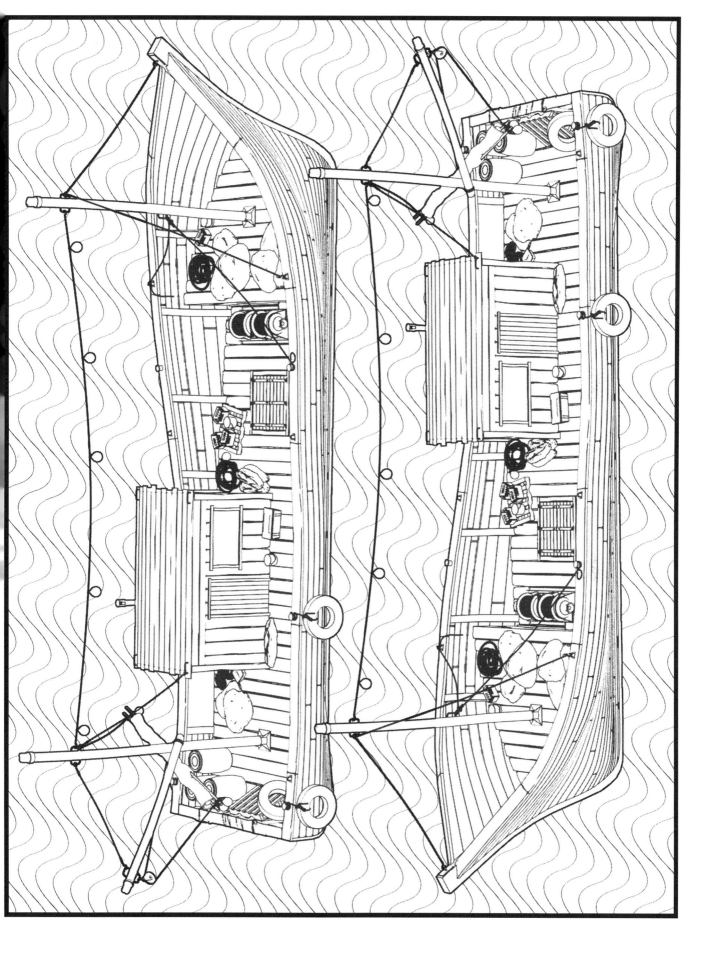

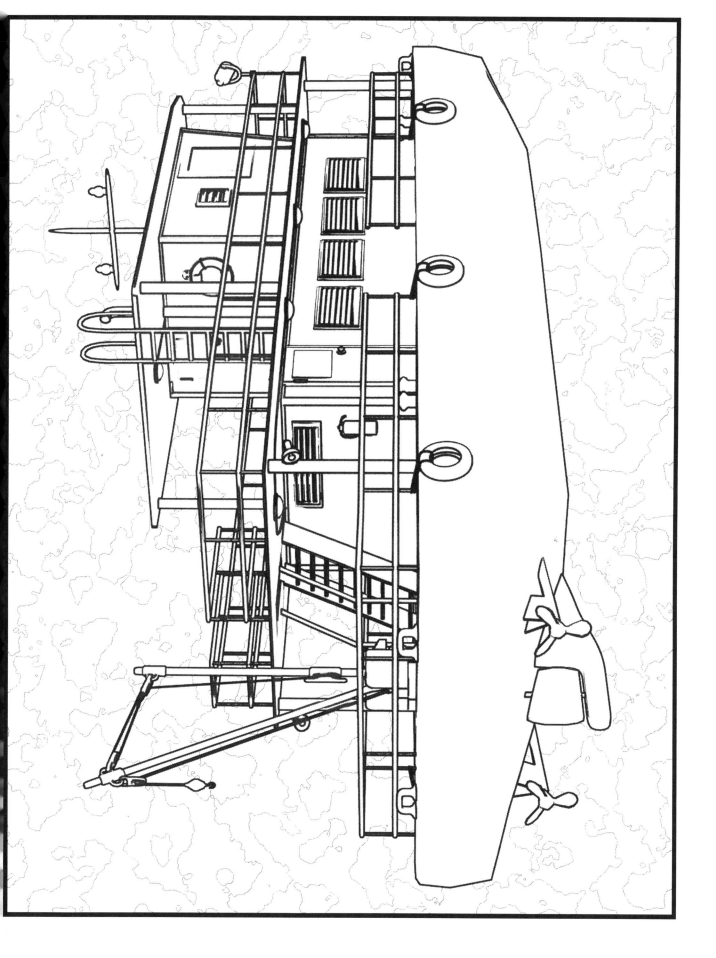

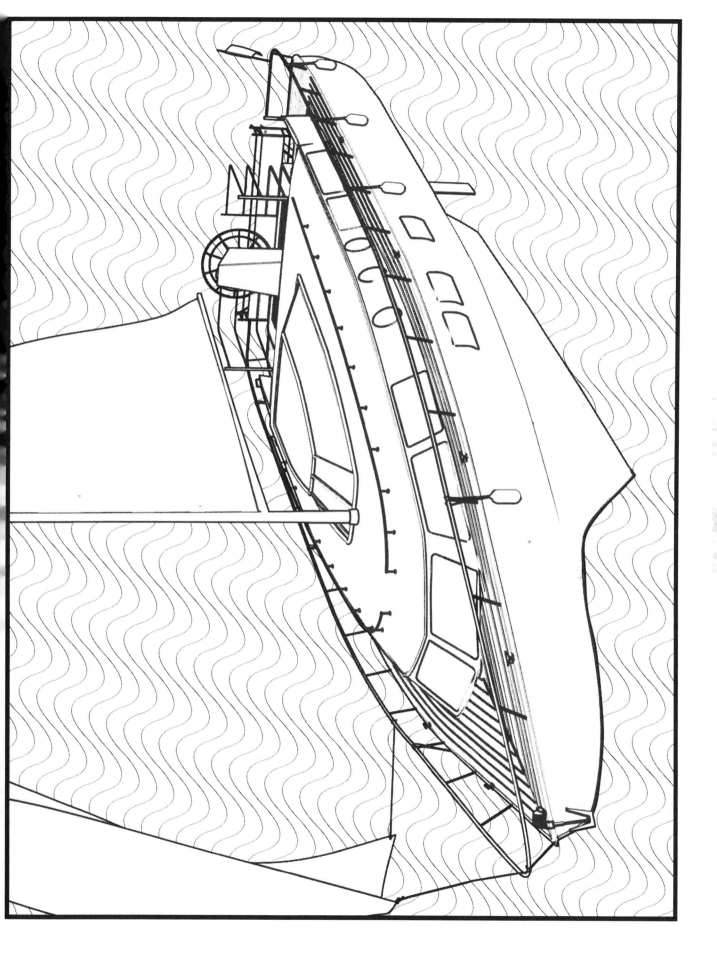

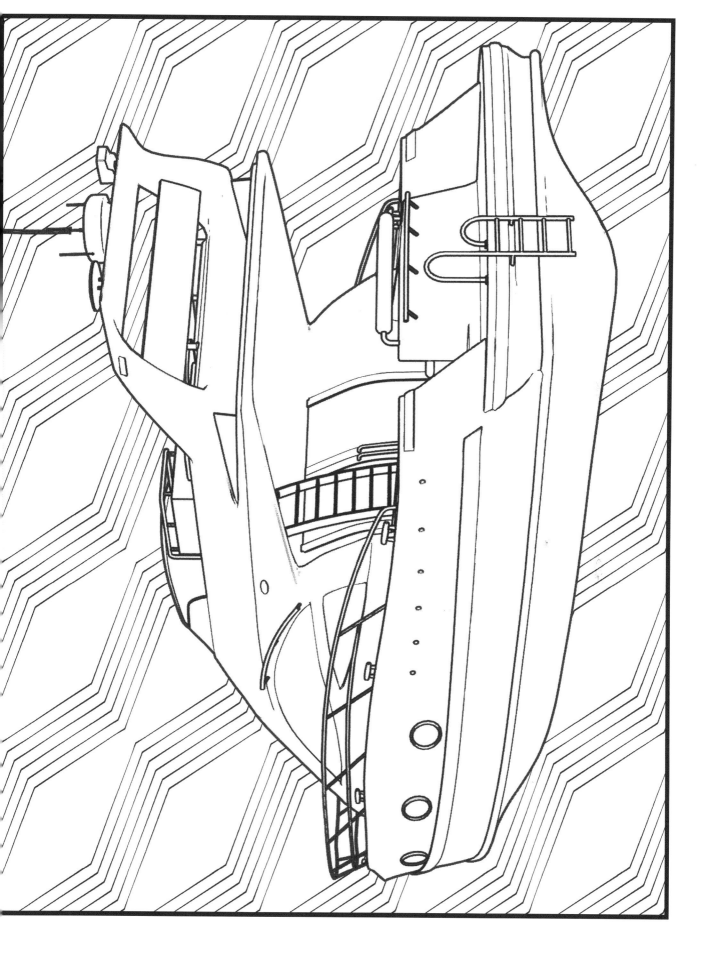

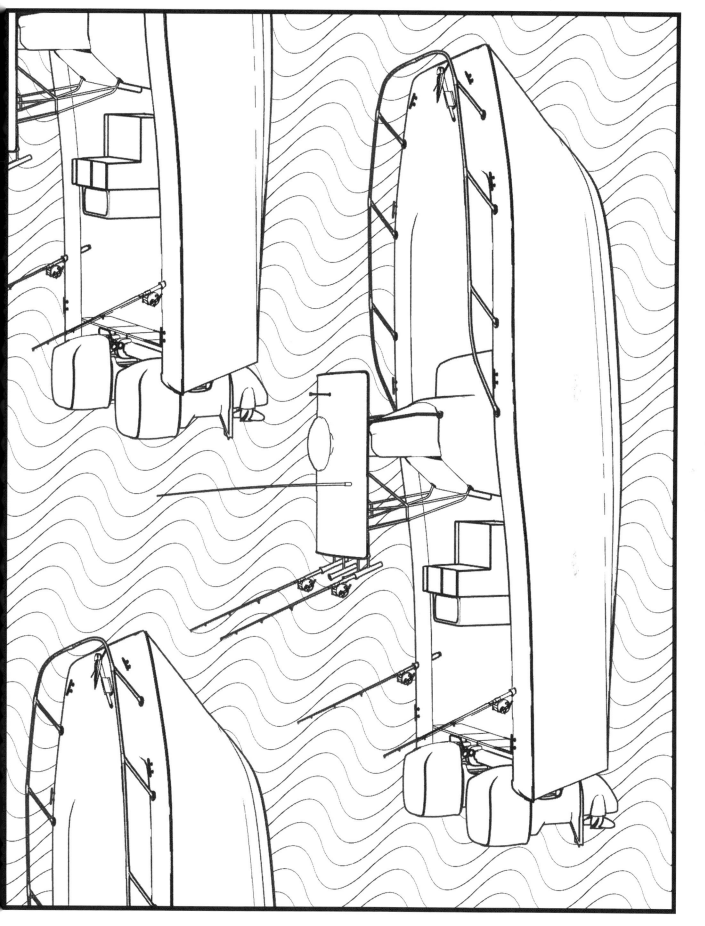

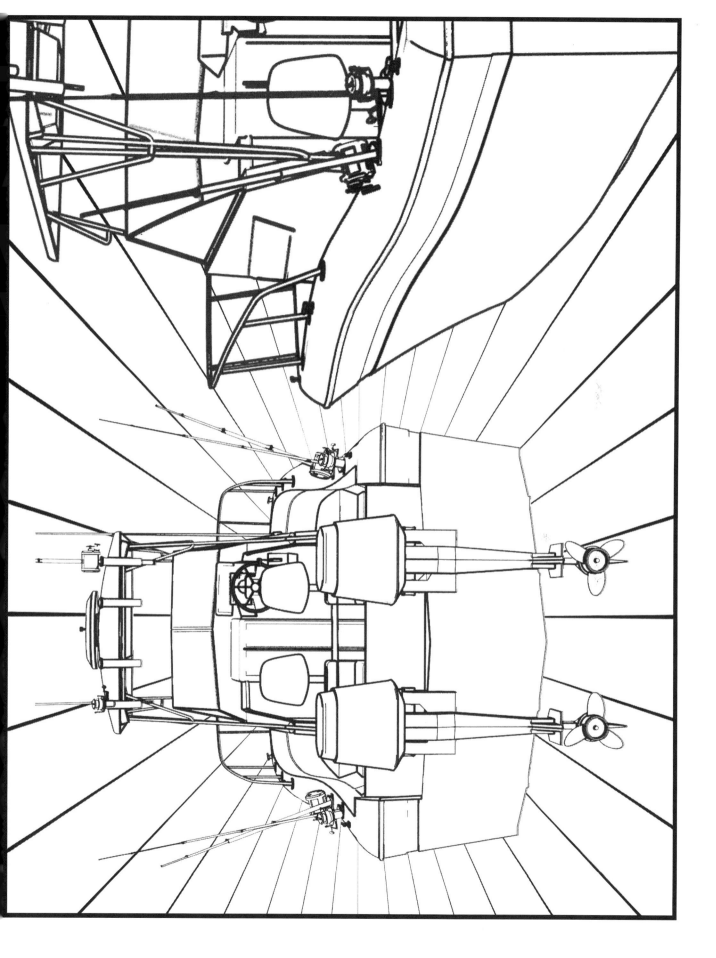

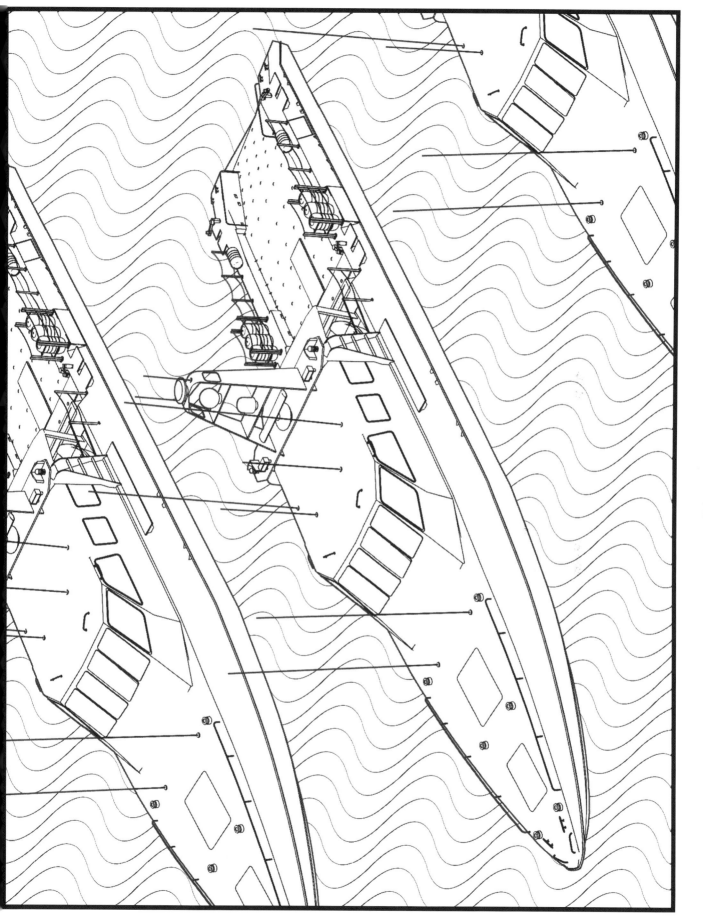

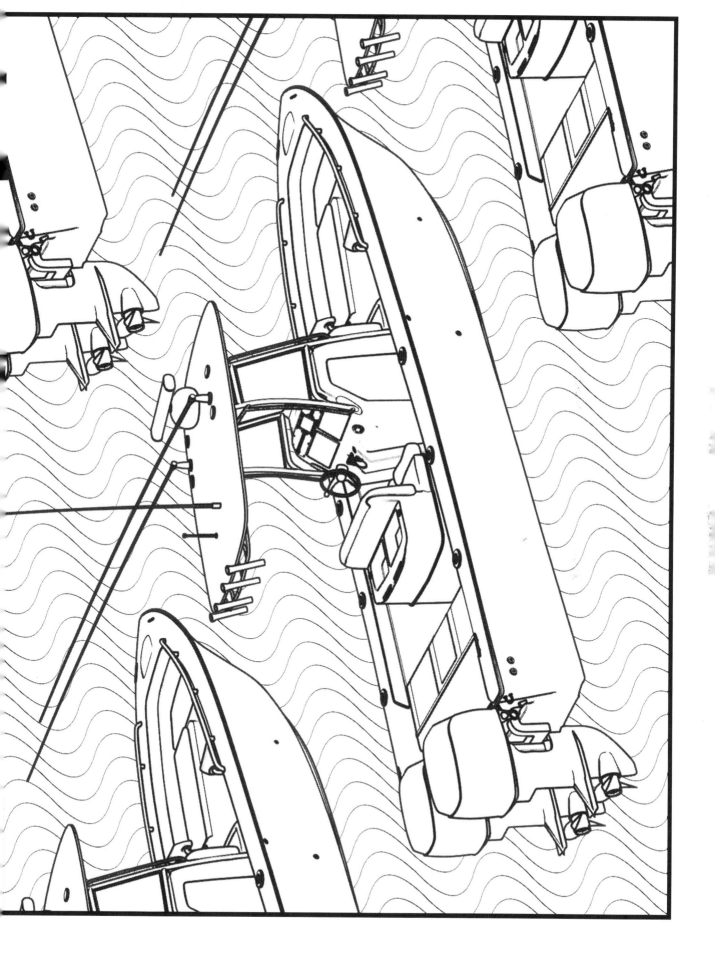

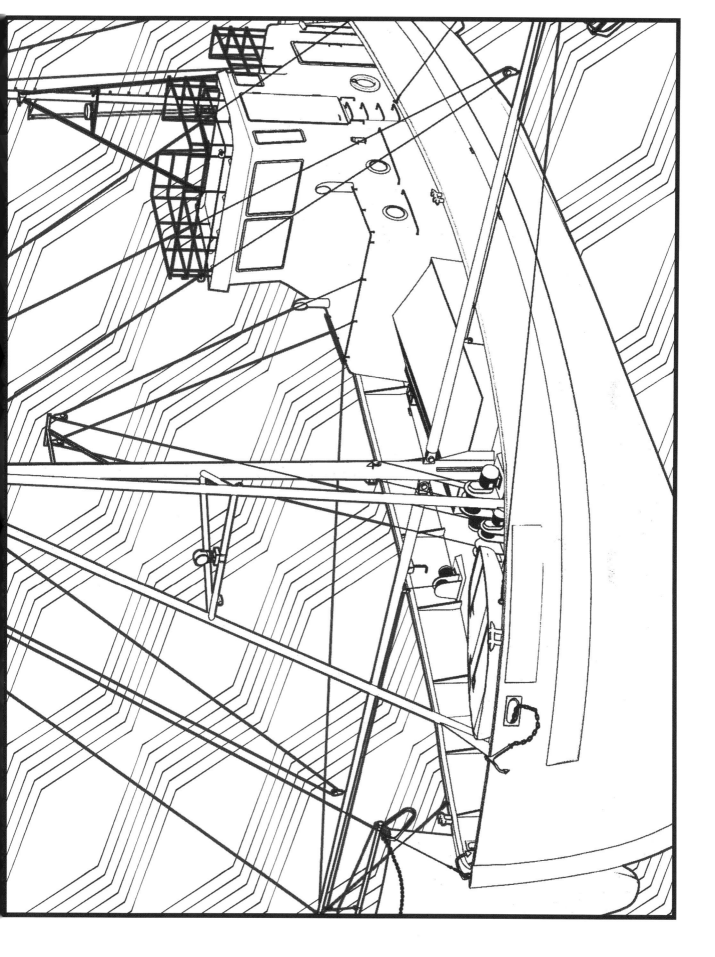

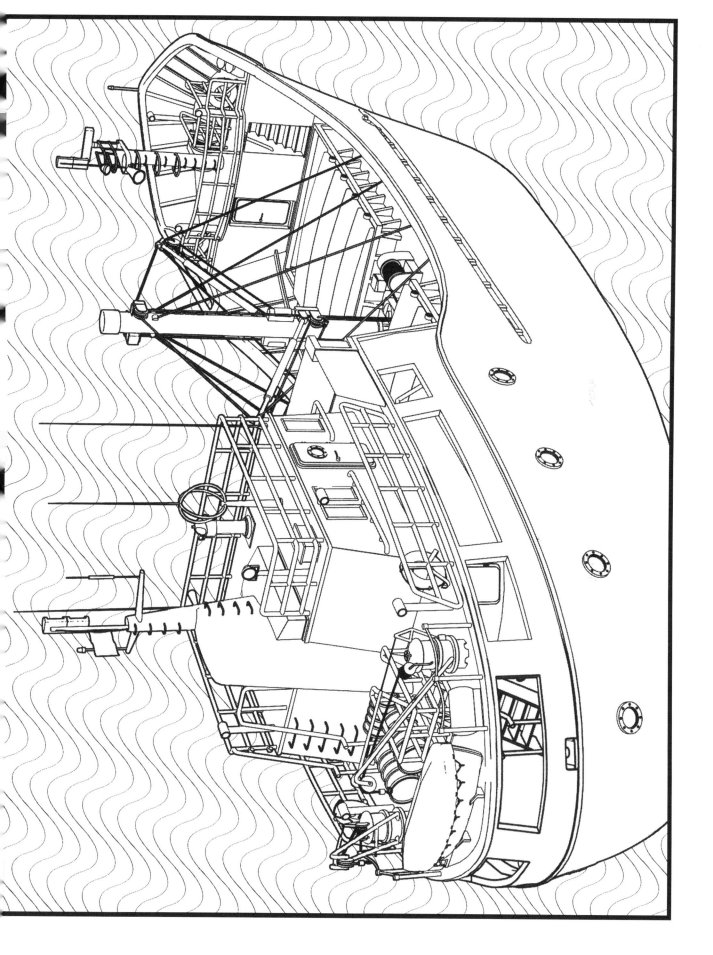

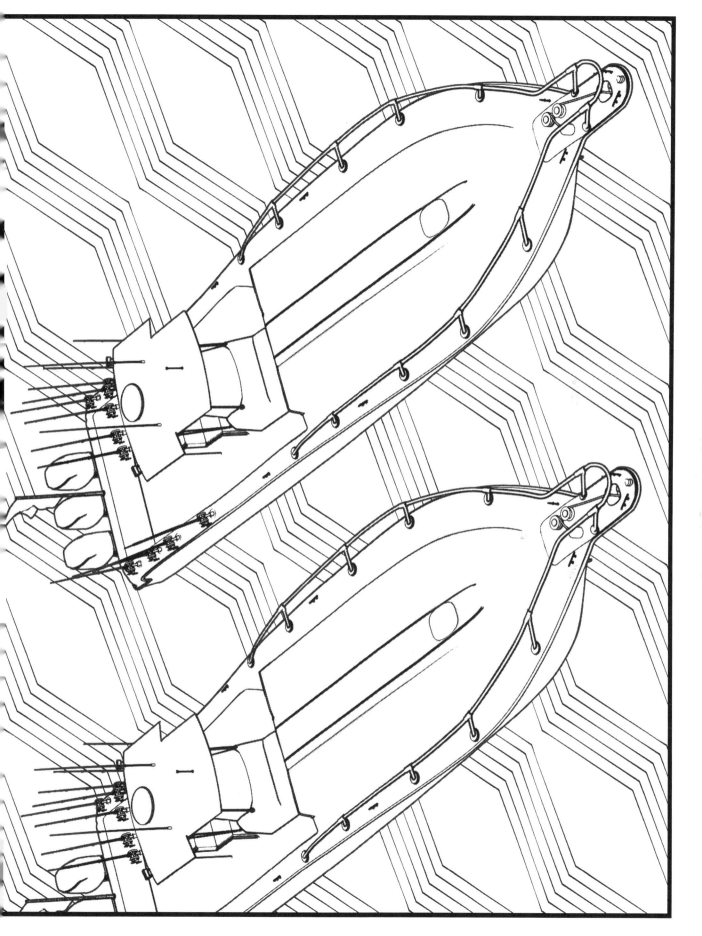

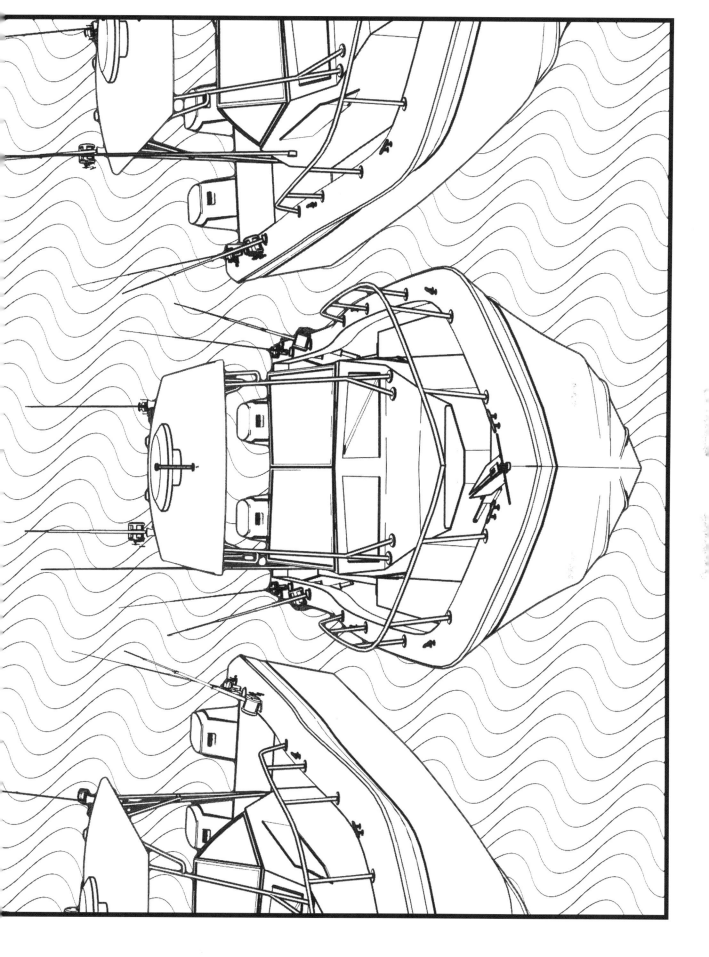

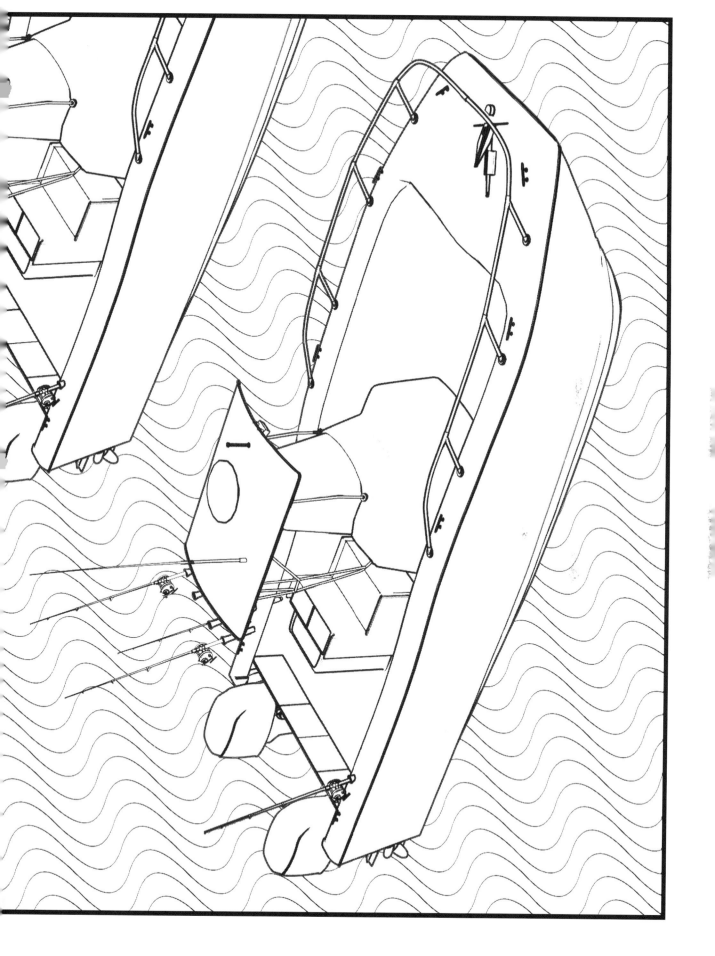

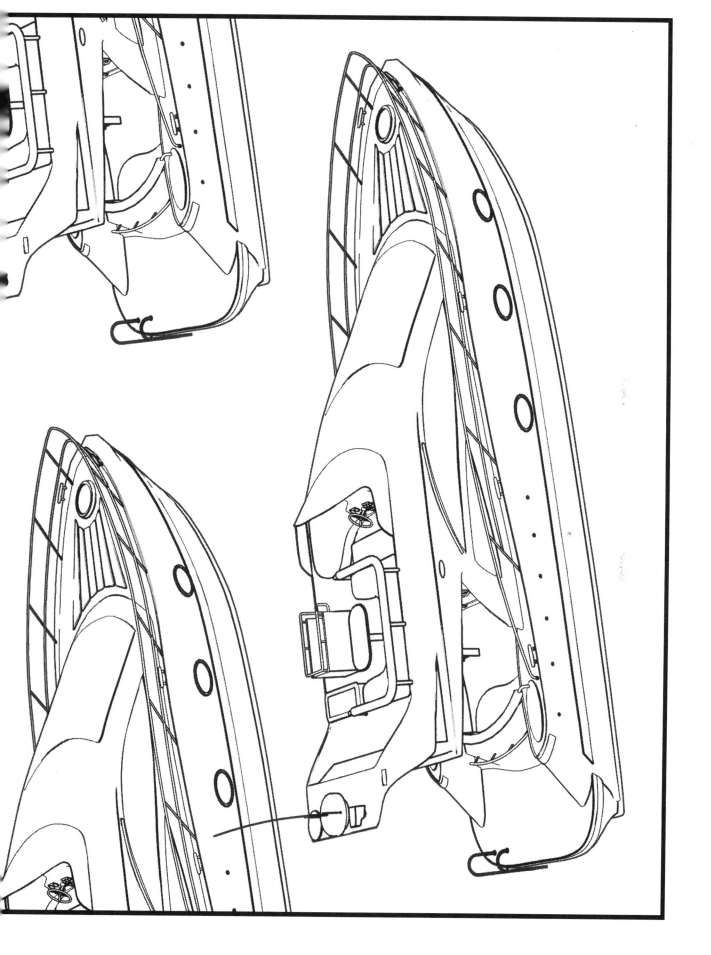

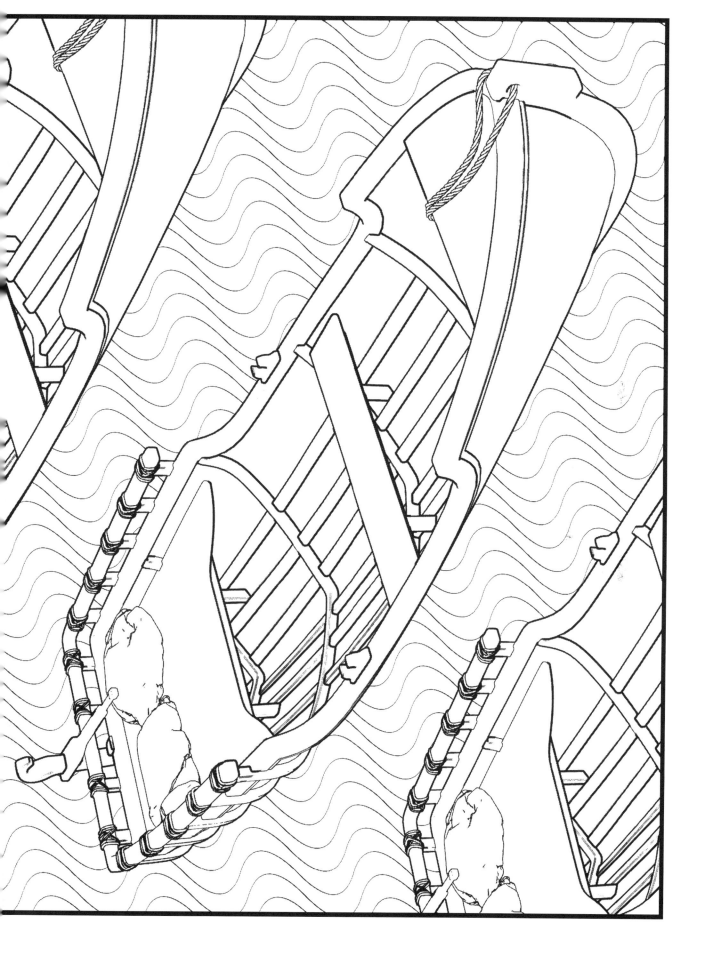

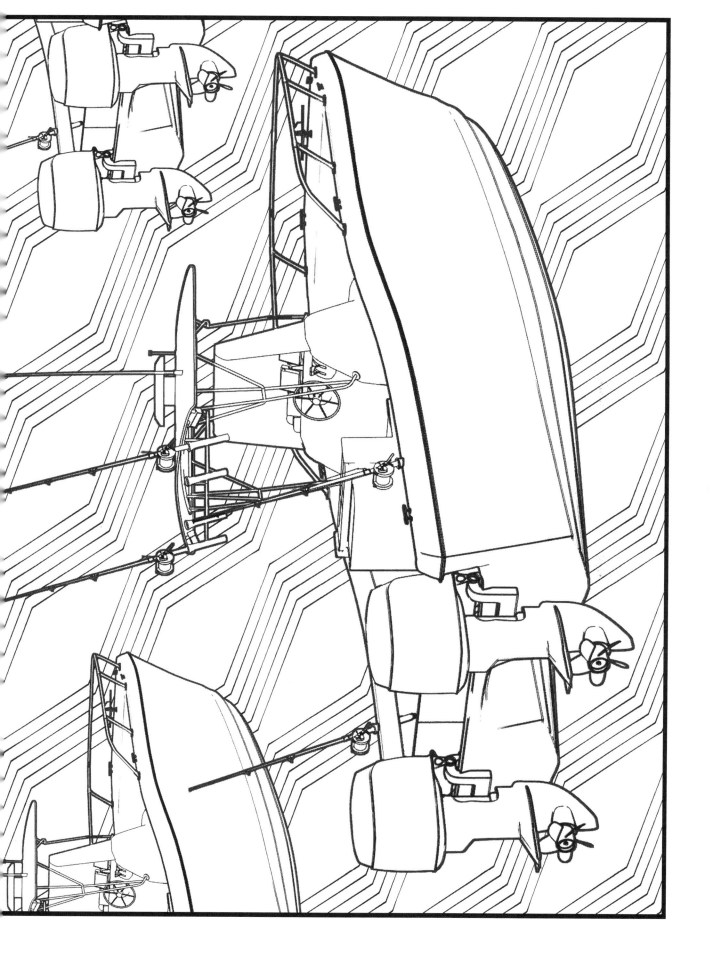

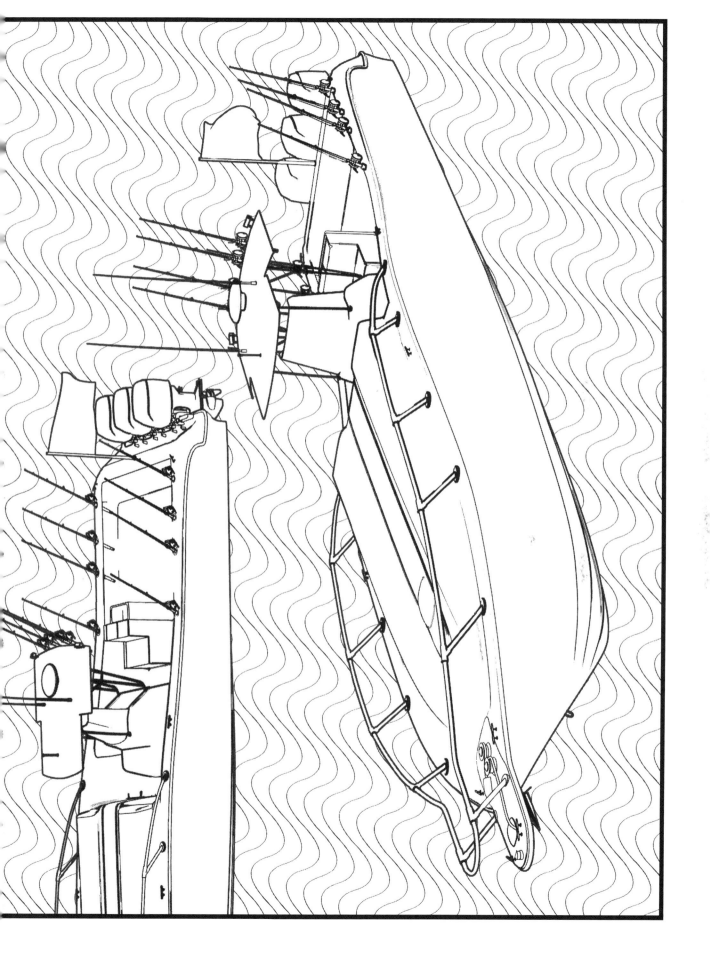

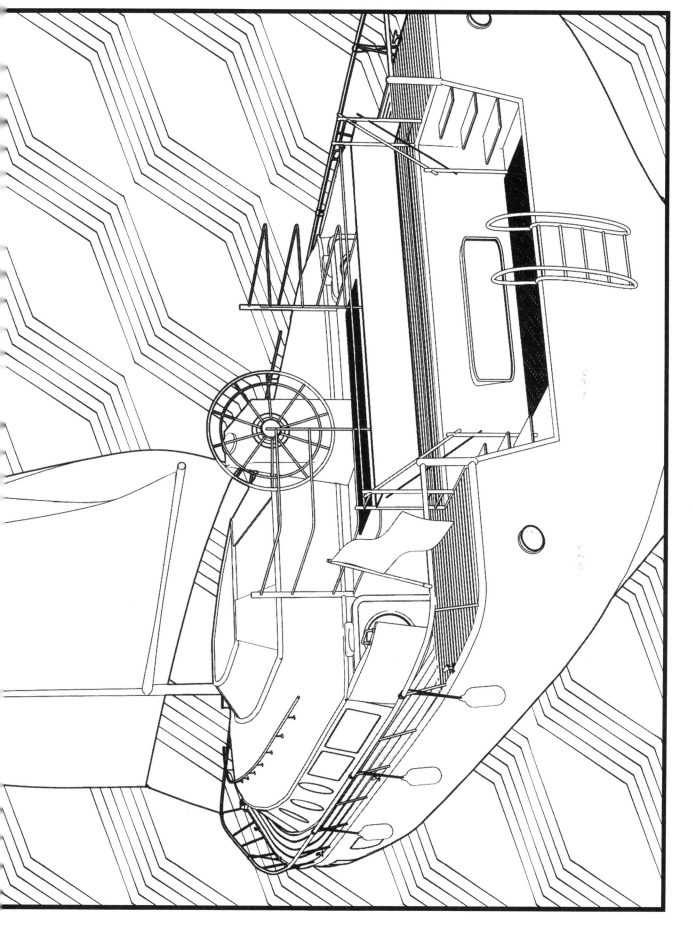

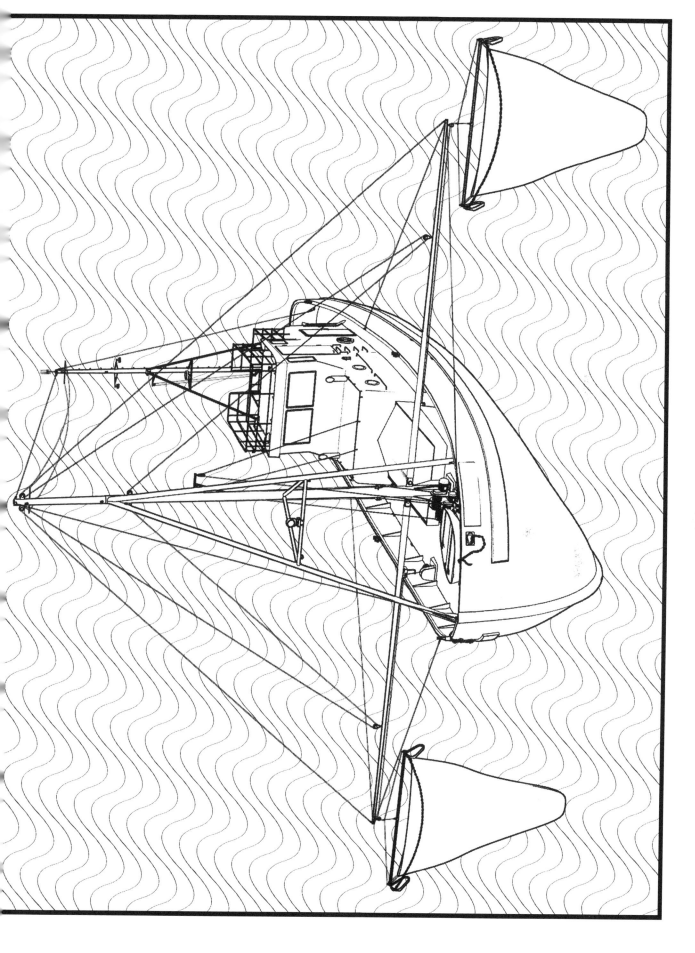

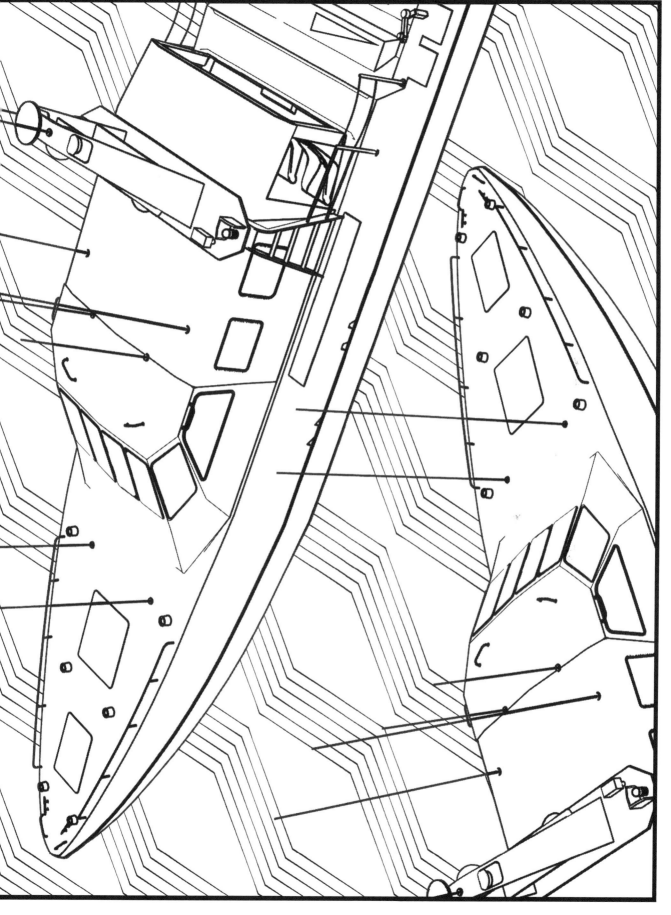

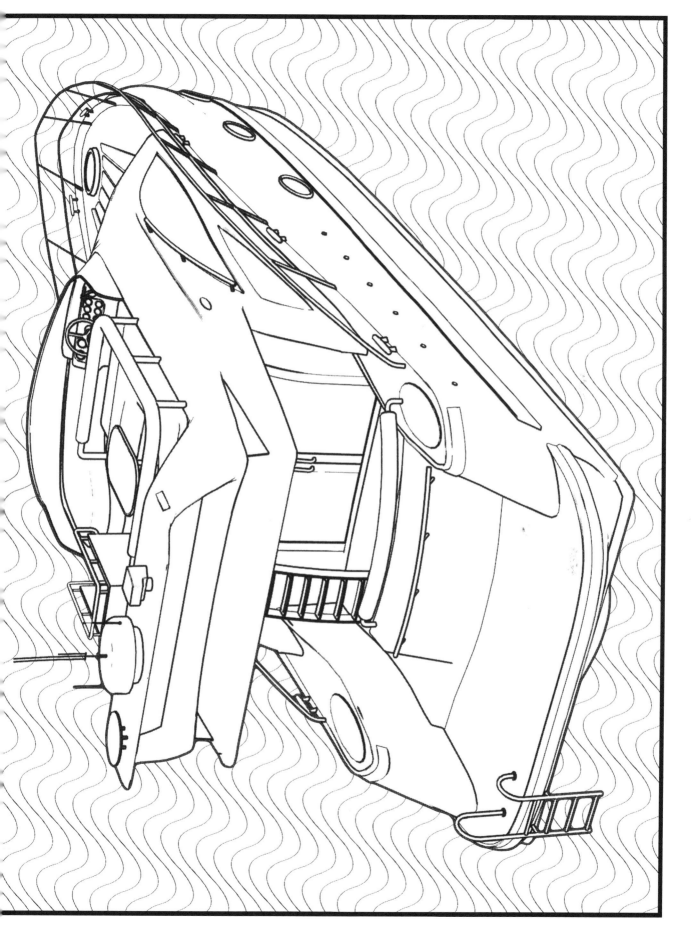

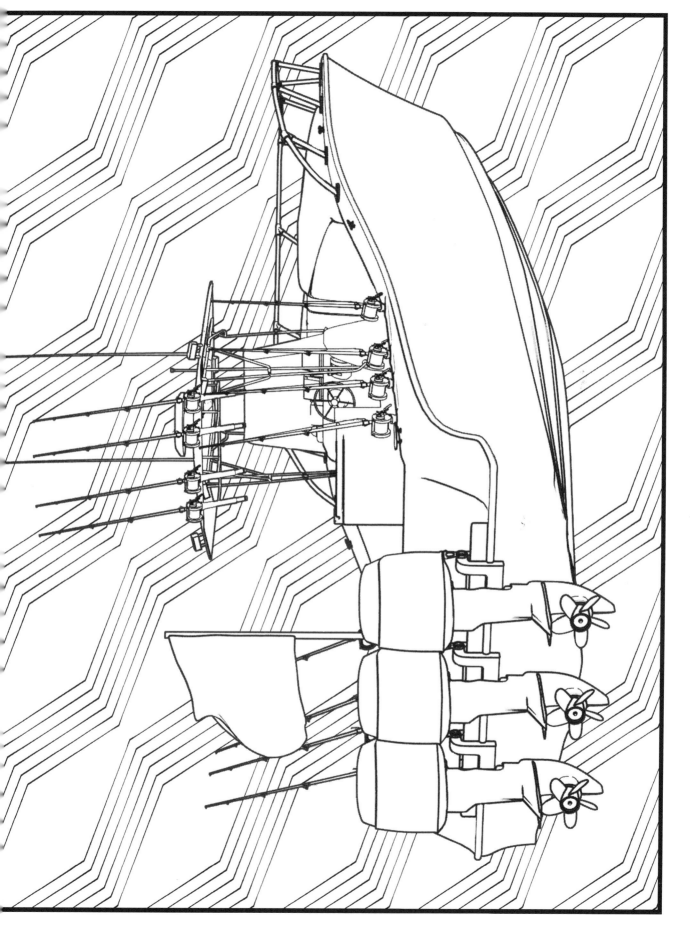

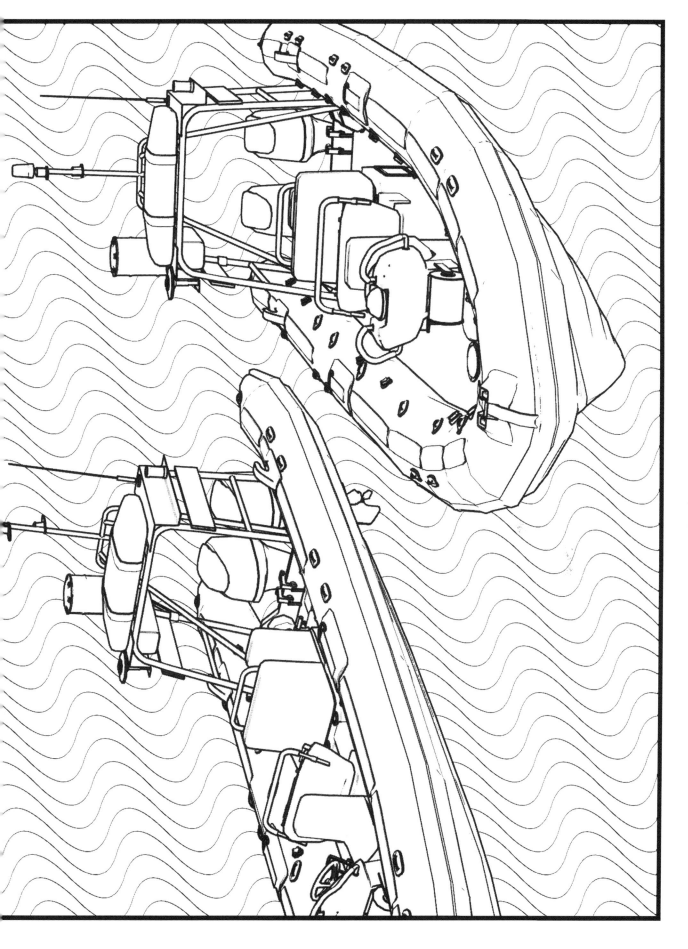

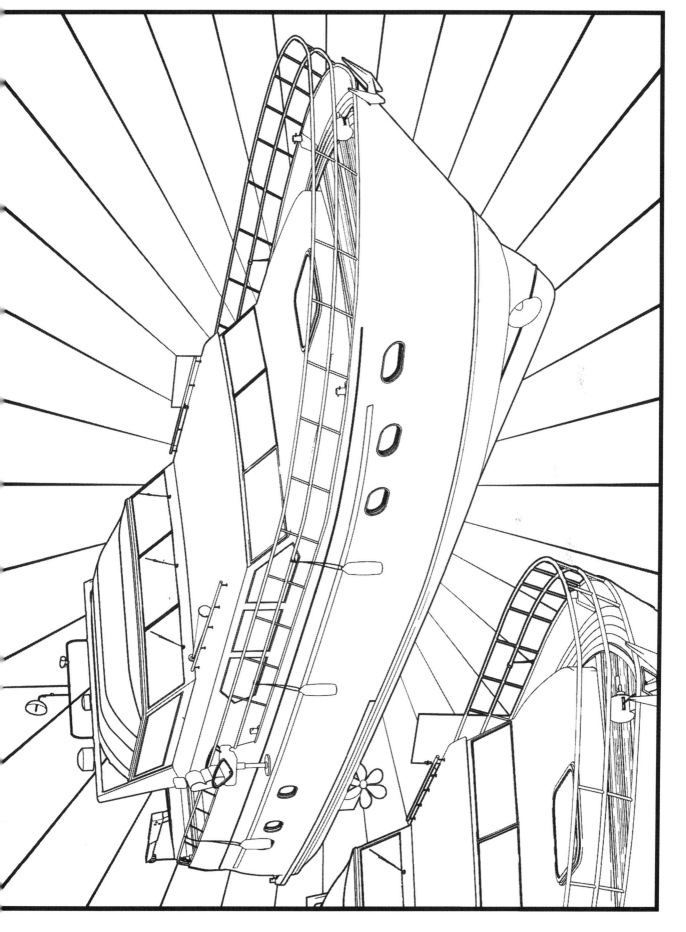

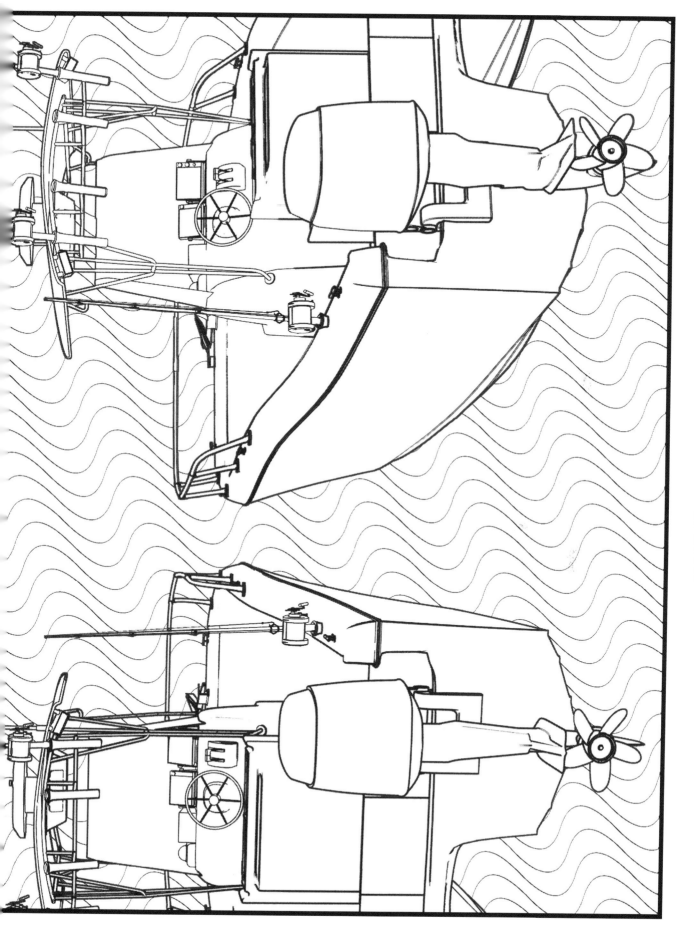

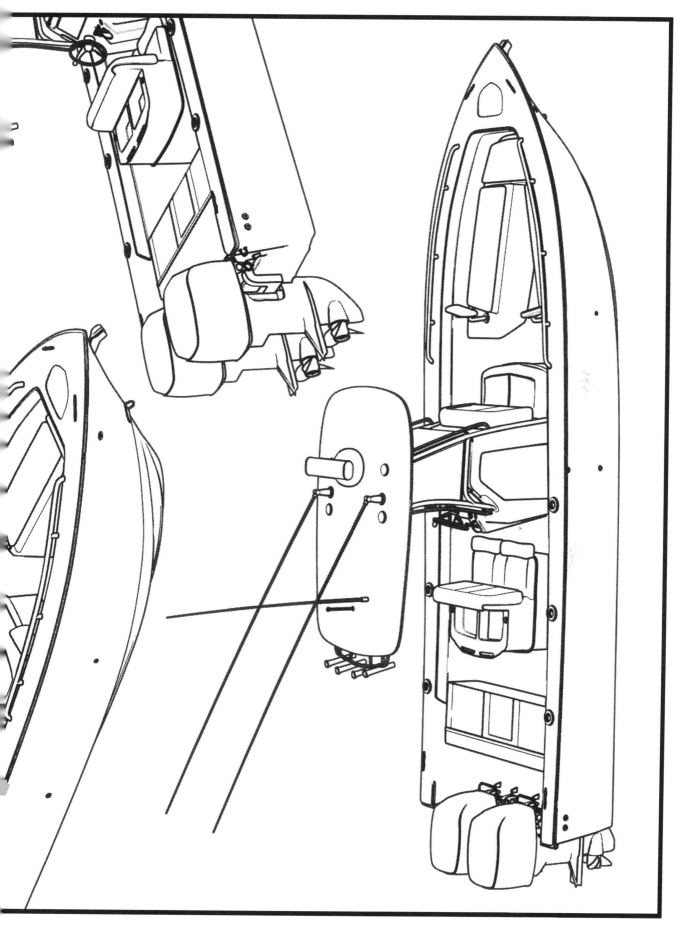

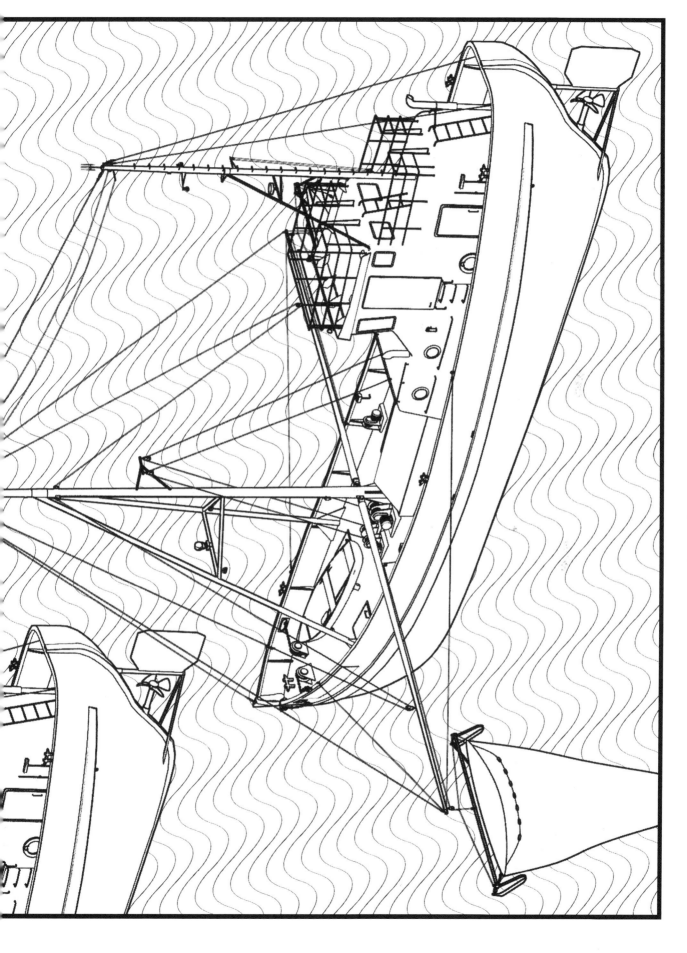

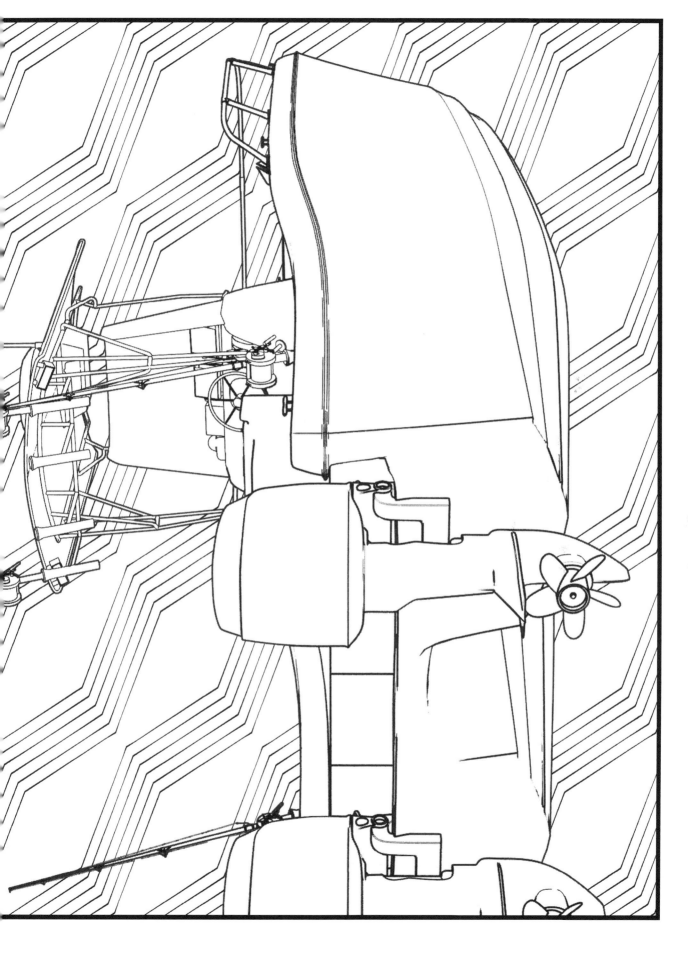

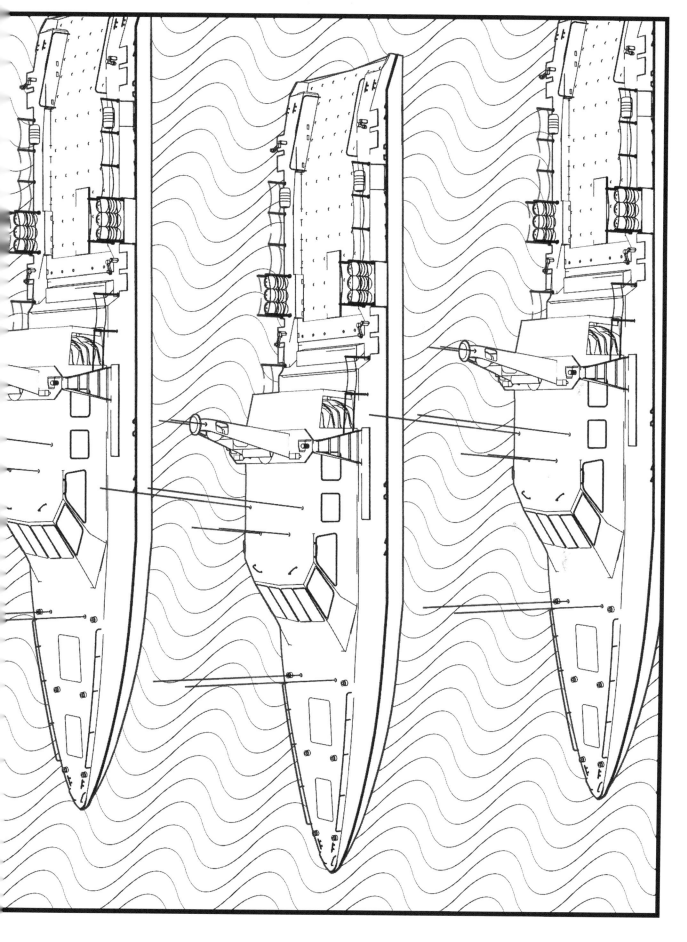

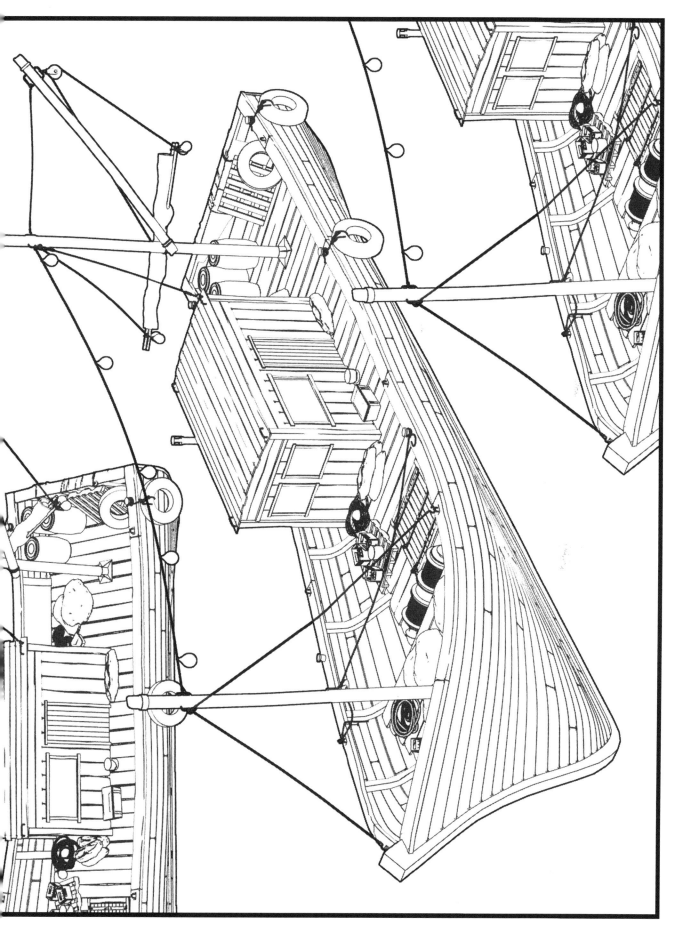

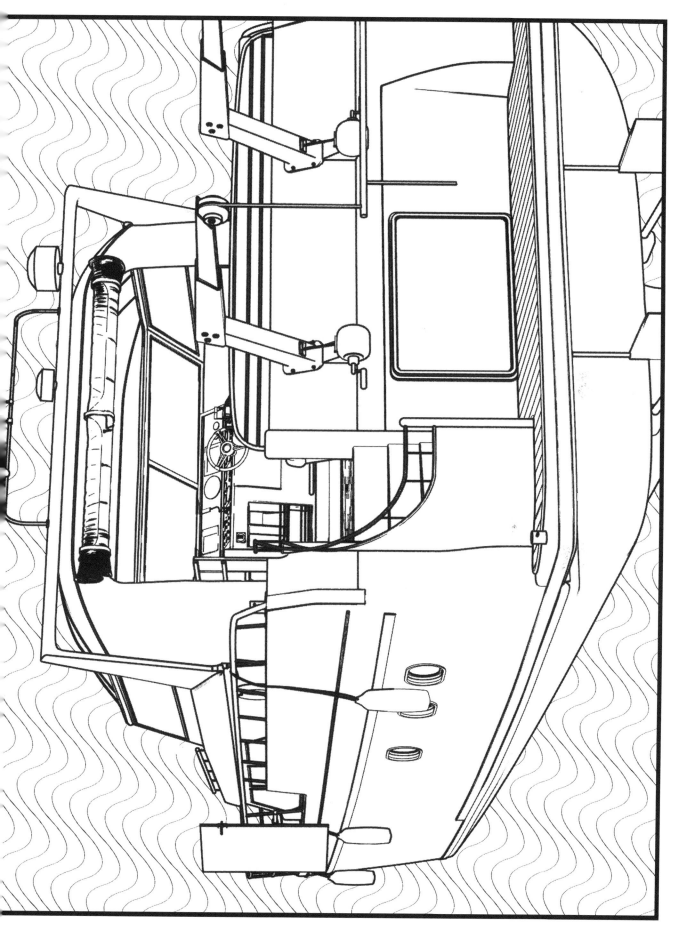

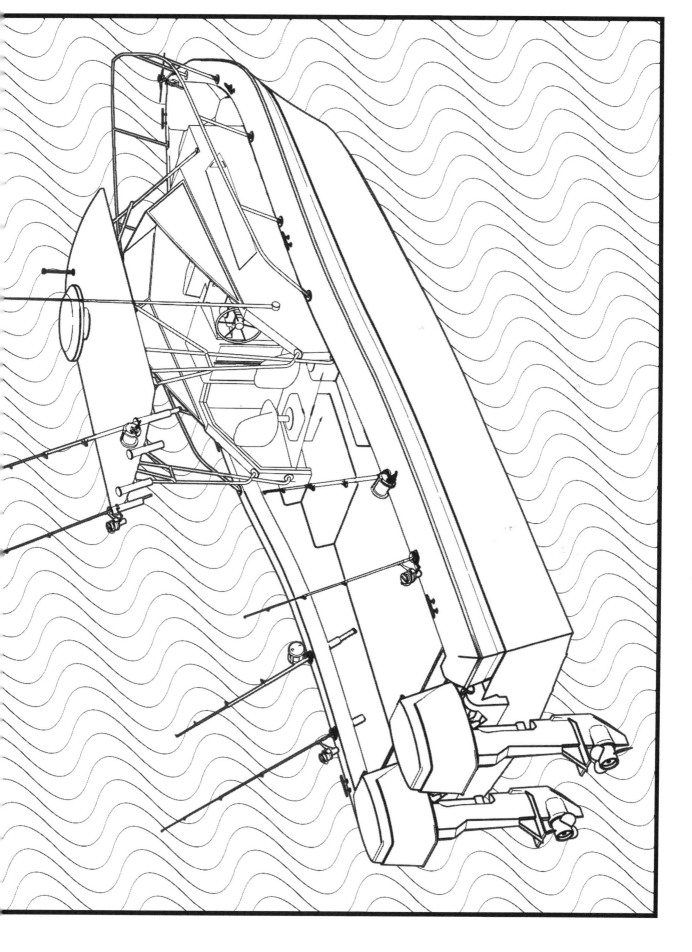

Made in the USA
Monee, IL
23 May 2023